IGNITE THE GENIUS WITHIN

IGNITE
THE GENIUS WITHIN

Discover Your Full Potential

DR. CHRISTINE RANCK AND CHRISTOPHER LEE NUTTER

DUTTON

DUTTON

Published by Penguin Group (USA) Inc.

375 Hudson Street, New York, New York 10014, U.S.A.

Penguin Group (Canada), 90 Eglinton Avenue East, Suite 700, Toronto, Ontario M4P 2Y3, Canada (a division of Pearson Penguin Canada Inc.); Penguin Books Ltd, 80 Strand, London WC2R 0RL, England; Penguin Ireland, 25 St Stephen's Green, Dublin 2, Ireland (a division of Penguin Books Ltd); Penguin Group (Australia), 250 Camberwell Road, Camberwell, Victoria 3124, Australia (a division of Pearson Australia Group Pty Ltd); Penguin Books India Pvt Ltd, 11 Community Centre, Panchsheel Park, New Delhi — 110 017, India; Penguin Group (NZ), 67 Apollo Drive, Rosedale, North Shore 0632, New Zealand (a division of Pearson New Zealand Ltd); Penguin Books (South Africa) (Pty) Ltd, 24 Sturdee Avenue, Rosebank, Johannesburg 2196, South Africa

Penguin Books Ltd, Registered Offices: 80 Strand, London WC2R 0RL, England

Published by Dutton, a member of Penguin Group (USA) Inc.

First printing, March 2009

10   9   8   7   6   5   4   3   2   1

 REGISTERED TRADEMARK—MARCA REGISTRADA

Library of Congress Cataloging-in-Publication Data has been applied for.

ISBN 978-0-525-95094-3

Printed in the United States of America
Set in Minion Pro with ITC Avant Garde Gothic
Designed by Daniel Lagin

To Rich, the brightest light in my universe.

—CHRISTINE RANCK

*To my brother Jason, who rescued me from myself on
more occasions than I can count.*

—CHRIS NUTTER

INTRODUCTION

We always get exactly what we want.

However, we are not *aware* of most of what we want. To make matters even more challenging, most of us are not even aware that we want all kinds of things we aren't conscious of. That is why there is so much disparity between what we think we want and what we actually get—why, for instance, we say we want more money but don't make it; why we say we want wonderful relationships but don't have them; why we claim we want to be happy but aren't.

There are a lot of reasons for this convoluted and universal condition.

To begin with, we have trained ourselves since childhood to believe that much of what happens in our lives happens *to us*. We then learn to attribute the disparity between what we want and what we actually get to the interference of some external force that is greater than us—an unfair world, an unfeeling universe, luck, God, biology, karma, the one that got away—and all we can do is react to it. Thus we unknowingly "project" our own power and our own hidden desires on to what we perceive as external forces that feel beyond our ability to control them. The fact that so many of our life experiences feel completely out of our control only reinforces our chronic sense of powerlessness.

Even though we are always masterminding our lives (we can't help but do so), we do it in large part unconsciously, unaware that everything that seems to be happening *to us* is actually the direct result of our own hidden desires. Not realizing that we are totally in the director's seat, we unwittingly use our power to create obstacles between ourselves and what would make us happy and fulfilled. Thus we remain convinced that we are helpless to overcome these mystifying barriers.

Though our will is always at work determining what we experience, our lack of conscious connection to our hidden power renders us incapable of making our will work for us rather than against us.

That is where this book comes in.

This book is an instrument to help you learn that there is no power in your life other than your own. The book will help you discover for yourself the source of your experiences—both good and bad—within your own mind. As you discover this, the possibility opens up that you contain potentially limitless power over your own life.

It accomplishes this through three mediums:

- **Images** of people, places, and things;
- **A soundtrack** that is known to help bring thoughts and feelings to the surface, calm the nervous system, and evoke dreamlike imagery. Instead of hearing stereo sound in both ears, you will notice that the sound undulates back and forth

from one side to the other. This "bilateral" stimulation of the brain will help to put you in a sort of waking dream state that, as in sleeping dreams, frees you up to travel through space and time without having to physically move; and

- Short, simple **instructions** that ask you to describe what is there in the image.

If you can describe what is there on the page, then you can see for yourself that the source of your experiences is in your own mind. After all, no picture in the universe has feelings and thoughts, and no image ever has had a meaning or a story without a person to give it one. So if you experience anything at all by looking at an image, you are experiencing a reflection of yourself.

As you discover yourself in the images, you will start to recognize yourself in the world and even the universe. This revolutionary realization will help you see that your obstacles are not the result of an external world keeping you down but are actually an expression of your own hidden desires. And if you make your obstacles, then you can also *un*make them. This discovery makes it conceivable that nothing is *fixed*, but rather that everything, including you, exists in a state of *possibility* and therefore can change.

This transition from a state of passivity into taking full responsibility for and power over your life is an "ah-ha!" moment that means living in one world one minute and living in a totally different one the next. And that is moving without moving. In science, moving to a different plane of existence without physically moving is called a "quantum leap," and it is something that you have the power to do because *quantum leaps can be entirely internal.* All it takes to make a quantum leap is the application of your full awareness on what you desire, and then simply watching it unfold . . . as it always has.

Recognizing your will at work in everything that happens in your life isn't easy. But the sense of disconnection between what you want and what happens does not change the truth about yourself. It does however keep you from *knowing* yourself. And the consequences of not knowing ourselves have made life difficult indeed. With so many of our desires hidden from view, the result is endless conflict in our lives. Uncovering your hidden desires helps you get out of conflict with yourself about what you want, helping you access the power to only want what will make you happy.

With this quantum leap of clarity, you might get exactly what you want right away, or simply an opportunity that will lead you there. But the real discovery is in seeing for yourself that the opportunity or result did not come to you from an external source, but came to you because you wanted it.

The other way this book will enable you to make a quantum leap will be through helping you connect to the dimensions of your mind that are *already* experiencing your heart's desires. This book is an instrument that will help you use your own awareness to see that everything you want to have, you already do; everywhere you want to go, you're already there; everything you want to be, you already are. You will see that there is no distance in time or space between you and what will make you happy . . . the only distance is in your ability to see it.

This quantum-leap approach to getting what you want out of life is the opposite of what we think of as "work."

It is much more akin to play, for it is a process of allowing rather than forcing; revealing rather than making. Once you get good at turning your attention inward to what you are making in your mind, changing your life in a substantial way can be as easy as getting up and moving into a different room. You realize you don't ever have to try to change anyone or anything else—all you have to do is change yourself, and everything else will follow.

Effortlessness as a means to experiencing the joy that comes from fulfilling your heart's desires is not a breakthrough concept. The Renaissance sculptor Michelangelo famously spoke about how he did not *create* David out of stone, but rather *revealed* David in the stone.

Creating something out of nothing is stressful and requires a lot of "work." Revealing something that is already there requires considerably less effort because it already exists. It's more like excavating than building. That is what we mean by effortlessness. The reason Michelangelo was able to see David already in the stone is that David was inside of *him.*

This premise is backed up by science, and this philosophy is a part of many belief systems. But to take it on faith in science or "spirituality" is to miss the point that it is *knowable.* After all, you do not have to believe in the ocean once you've seen one for yourself and jumped in. When that happens, belief is replaced with something much more precious: direct knowledge of your own power.

This power is the true source of creativity, and it is not something exclusive to artists or geniuses. When we say "Ignite the genius within," we are talking about discovering that you are already an artistic genius . . . you have been all along . . . for your whole life, both the good and the bad, is your own creation. When you understand this, you will see that creativity is rather an expression of your own power to turn every moment of your life into a beautiful piece of art.

From there, your experience of the world transmutes from one that keeps you from doing what you want to do, to one that is helping you out at every turn . . . because that is what you *want* it to do.

HOW TO GET THE MOST FROM THIS BOOK

The first thing to know when it comes to using this book is to not think of it as a book *about* anything for you to read and either believe or not believe.

Rather, think of it as a *mirror* that dramatically expands your knowledge of yourself. In doing so, you will become more aware of who you are; clearer about what you want; and more able to *only* want what will make you happy. The result will be less conflict in your life and greater ease when it comes to being able to simply enjoy it.

Here's how to go about it:

1. **Go to www.ignitethegeniuswithin.com and download the soundtrack.**

2. **Put earphones on and play the soundtrack** with the volume level loud enough for you to recognize distinct sounds, but soft enough so that it comes through mostly as background. The sound effects will alternate from your left ear to

your right ear, putting you in a relaxed, waking dream state that will help you recognize yourself in the images more easily. (And you must use earphones, not speakers, for the sounds to do their job.)

3. **Flip the book to any page and start there.** As you flip, you will be drawn to certain images, uninterested in others, and even averse to some. It is up to you which one you choose to stop on at any time. Just follow your instincts. That said, if you have a strong reaction one way or another to any image, you can be sure that there is something very big there for you to see.

4. **Follow the instructions laid out on the page.**
   Though the specific instructions will differ on every page, the same guidelines apply. With the sound on:

- Take in the image for as long as you like.
- Read the first instruction or question. (If there is none, simply take in the image.)
- Close your eyes and allow your mind to wander off. Don't *try* to do anything. Just daydream and free-associate using the images and the questions as a starting place, and let whatever happens happen for however long you want it to happen. Wander around "inside" yourself. Trust that whatever comes to mind is relevant. (When we say, "Go in," "Go inside," or "See where that takes you," this is what we mean.)
- Whenever you are ready, open your eyes. If there are further instructions, follow the same procedure again.

Though the images and instructions are different on every page, the same basic principle applies: *Do not do any work.*

In fact, your immediate reaction is usually the most relevant and most real, and it requires no work at all. From that point, just sit back and watch what memories, feelings, and experiences come up. Take your time. Embrace *everything* that comes to mind. As with a conventional mirror, all you have to do is look in and see what's there.

Note: Not every page is an exercise. Some pages have no images, and ask that you pay attention only to what you see in your mind in response to a statement or a question. Also included are essays to help you understand the process and yourself better. In either case, you will not find information to believe or not believe but rather signposts pointing the way toward greater understanding of yourself. But it is up to you what this greater understanding will be.

Here are the important things you need to know:

No matter what the question, *there is no wrong answer.* Every response (be it descriptive, physical, emotional, or visceral) is right. In fact, if you show a page to someone else, you will likely find that what each of you sees and how you respond are very different. You will also find that your responses to the images will change over time. The point of observing this is to help you realize that every reaction you have is absolutely correct.

There is no order. You are free to do and experience any part or parts of the book as you like when you like. You should follow any impulse you have to stop on or pass by a particular page. This book is designed to work best for you and you alone.

You don't have to finish a particular page. If you feel stuck or uncomfortable, move on. Find another page you are drawn to and go there instead. Go back to the first page whenever you're ready. Sometimes what you discover about yourself from another exercise will help you to move further with the troublesome page.

Do not judge what comes up. You may be in for some surprises. Some of them might not feel so good right away. And you simply may not like how they look or feel. But the thoughts and feelings that make us uncomfortable are often the very source of what blocks us. So stay open.

You cannot finish this book. Every time you look at something, you will see something new. Every time you see something new you will change. And every time you change you will see the image differently. So instead of thinking of this book as something to complete, think of it as infinitely renewable.

You are not learning about anything else but you. We traditionally approach learning from the standpoint that we are studying something or someone else. That is not the case here. No matter what or who it seems you see, you are only ever learning about yourself.

But the main thing to know about this mirror you hold in your hands is that it does not require force or effort to make it work. Instead it requires a release from effort altogether, and the trust that everything that happens is exactly right. Because everything about you is exactly right. In that condition you will discover what you truly long for . . . and find that it was waiting for you all along.

IGNITE THE GENIUS WITHIN

This is a pond of pure possibility that can be turned into absolutely anything.

Close your eyes and picture this pond.

Then think of something, anything at all.

Watch that thought, and any other thoughts, come down like rain, creating the ripples on this pond.

Pick one thought and let it open up like one of the ripples. Go where it takes you as if you are riding the edge of the ripple. Notice the images and feelings that come up. Notice how real the whole experience looks and feels.

Start off with any thought at all that you can catch in your daily life.

Instead of allowing that thought to ripple out without examination, stop and ask yourself:

Do you want the reality that thought produces?

If you don't, pause, and say, "I don't have to make that thought anymore."

Then ask yourself, "What do I want instead?"

Let a new thought that expresses that desire open up, and

imagine the ripple going out on the pond. Every time you catch the old thought, let it go, and concentrate on the new one.

Do this as many times as it takes.

Wait and watch what the new thought produces.

Every day your thoughts rain down onto the pond of possibility, rippling out.

Contained within each ripple is an entire experience in your mind—the feelings, the sights, the sounds, the outcomes, all of it.

The entirety of an experience contained within a single thought is an example of what is called a **hologram**. This is a word to describe a part—in this case a thought—that contains within it the whole—in this case, the experience.

But the power of thought doesn't stop there. As each thought radiates out in your mind, it eventually finds an expression of itself in your life, such as in the form of a person, an event, or a thing. Realizing this, you can begin paying these thoughts very close attention.

The soundtrack you are hearing is designed to gently help you get into a relaxed state. The sounds oscillate from one ear to the other in order to alternately stimulate both lobes of your brain. This back-and-forth auditory stimulation distracts it from the nonstop chatter that we call "thinking" ("I can't believe he did that to me!" "I need to wash my car," "I'll never be able to pay my bills") but is really just noise that makes it very difficult to hear, or think, anything else. Startling your brain off the treadmill of repetitive and pointless mental *activity* puts it in a state of *receptivity* to see and experience more than what you are usually aware of. (If you've ever been startled by an unexpected event, like a car suddenly moving into your lane, and you immediately stopped "thinking," then you know what we're talking about.)

The sound effects also help pull memories to the surface, and evoke a state not unlike the one you experience in your sleeping dreams or daydreams, where you can revisit your past, envision possibilities, and travel anywhere in the universe you like without being restricted by the limits of time and space.

Listening to the soundtrack while focusing on the images in these pages makes it considerably easier to snap out of your habitual daily reality and enter a realm where you can be anywhere or anything you can imagine, as you do in your dreams. Now, you are awake, and conscious of what's happening. In this wakened dream-state you sail above your standard, daily reality. You can see with greater clarity the parts of you that are stuck in old, limited, and damaging ways of thinking, and connect more easily to a future free from the fears and limits that bind you.

So what has seemed like it was far away or far removed can be experienced in an instant in your mind because you are already there. And changing what you imagine is the first step to changing what you experience in your life. That's what this soundtrack will help you do.

Forget what you know.

How does she feel?

Close your eyes and see what comes to mind.

Allow yourself to rest in this feeling for however long you like.

Is this creativity?

If you weren't guilty, how would you feel?

If you weren't worried,
what would you do?

If you trusted yourself,
what possibilities would you see?

Think of a younger you.

If you could do anything for them, or say anything to them,
what would it be?

Close your eyes and see what happens.

It was technically impossible for the person responsible for this pyramid to build it from the ground up because he did not have access to the bottom of the sand pile. Instead, he had to reveal it from the top down. So he didn't make the pyramid—he discovered it. It was a process of excavation, not building.

If so, was the pyramid already there? Or was it only there when he started looking for it? Go inside.

Think of something you want. Now, imagine that it is already there and only has to be revealed. Close your eyes and see where that takes you.

Is there a hidden side of the moon?
If you can't see it, how do you know it's there?
Just because you can't see it doesn't mean it isn't there.
So could it be that there is more to you than just what you can see?
Close your eyes and see where you go.

From the Earth, we always see the same side of the Moon. In all of human history, we have never seen the other side from Earth because, as it revolves around us, the Moon is also turning in perfect precision along with the Earth's rotation so that the same side is always showing, and the other side is always hidden. The purpose of this particular cosmic mystery is unknown.

What is this man doing?

How do you feel about him?

Close your eyes and answer the question.

Put yourself in his place in the picture.

Close your eyes and try to imagine the top of the tree moving into your arm's reach.

Once you've done this, see how you feel about it, and notice if you have any sensations in your body.

Now try imagining the tree top moving farther away.

Is there anything in either situation that feels familiar or surprises you?

With this insight in mind, close your eyes and let your mind wander.

What do you notice?

What are you proud of?

Think of something mysterious that you can't explain.
Go inside, and see where that leads you.

Judging what you want as "wrong," such as because it is selfish, or sinful, or irresponsible, or because you don't deserve it, keeps you from getting or being what you want.

Not getting what you want keeps you from learning that you always get, and become, what you want.

Not learning that you get and become what you want keeps you from being able to want or be anything greater.

What are the odds of both dice coming up sixes?

Now picture them in the air, and answer the question.

Decide how you want the dice to roll.

Close your eyes and imagine throwing the dice.

Concentrate on seeing the dice roll like you want them to roll.

Practice this until you get better at deciding which way they land.

And notice how great it feels when they land the way you want them to.

The next time you find yourself at the mercy of "odds"—such as finding a parking space, encountering a long line, getting a job—close your eyes, picture the dice again, and visualize the dice coming up the way you want.

Realize that you decide the outcome.

Focus on the feeling of power that gives you.

Then, just as you practiced with the dice, imagine getting the outcome that you want in the specific situation you face.

Pay attention to the results you get.

Wherever you are right now, take a look around you. How many things do you see?

Now, take a look at this image. How many things do you see?

Wherever you are right now, you are also somewhere in this image. Notice how your perspective on the questions changes the answers. Go inside and contemplate that.

Where is your safe place?
Go in.

Do these fish know they are surrounded by water?
Go in and see where that takes you.

This is an image of a red "supergiant" star, which gave off a sudden pulse of light that illuminated everything around it that was normally dark.

Close your eyes and see if you can think of a time when an idea—whether it was yours or someone else's—illuminated everything and everyone around it.

See where that takes you.

NO!

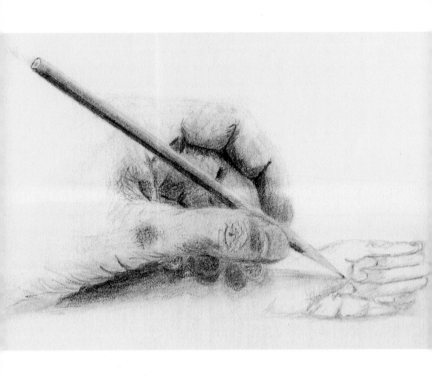

Who is doing the drawing?

Take in the image, close your eyes, and see what comes up.

Is it possible that you are doing the drawing?

Close your eyes and see where that takes you.

Have you ever had an idea that hit you like lightning? Close your eyes and think of a time.

Go in and rewind back to the moment it struck you. What were you doing?

Go back even further and recall the moment you identified the need for an idea.

Looking at this process, could it be that "intelligence" and "knowledge" are things you tune in to rather than something you are or have? In other words, could it be that simply identifying the need was like putting up a lightning rod that attracted the idea that came to you?

Go inside and see what comes up.

Can you escape freedom?

What if you were the sun?

And you looked down and saw a beautiful sun looking back at you.

You wouldn't know it was a reflection.

You would think it was a beautiful sun that you discovered.

But the "sun" you see wasn't there until you looked at it.

So you both discovered the "sun" and *made* this sun simultaneously.

Therefore this sun that you see is both something you made, and a reflection.

And it wasn't there until you looked at it.

Your whole world—every person you know, every event you observe, every memory you've got, everything you can see—is a result of the same process:

You see it, you make it, and you discover it, all at the same time. And it wasn't there before.

Because it is all a reflection of you.

Think about it.

Does she know how old she is?

Close your eyes, picture her,
and ask yourself the question again.

Does she know how old you are?
Close your eyes again and answer the question from her
perspective.

What if you didn't know how old you are?
Close your eyes and see where that takes you.

What is her story?

What comes easy to you?
What do you love to do?
When do you have the most fun?
Go in.

We have been trained to ignore or dismiss what we love to do, and to seek out our answers in what is hard to do. But the answer to what you seek is actually found in what comes easiest; what you have fun doing; what you love to do. From there your inspiration, your creativity, your passion, come naturally, and without effort. When you're in that state the world brings to you all the help you need . . . and if you feel you have lost it, or don't know anymore what you love to do, trust that it is never too late to get it back.

When you look at yourself in a broken mirror, you see that each piece has its own view of you.

This perfectly reflects the condition we find ourselves in today. Though it is not widely recognized, the fact is that our *selves*—which is to say our personalities, our identities, our very consciousness—are shattered into many pieces. Like a broken mirror, each one has its own view of itself with a unique set of wants, beliefs, and expectations. In fact, each one has its own "personality."

This is not something you have to believe or not believe. But it is something that can easily be observed if you keep your eyes open for it.

For instance, anytime you wanted to stay home and play on a beautiful day but you knew you had to get to the office, or you wanted to buy something frivolous and fun but forced yourself to save the money, you experienced the conflicted longings between a part of you that is a child, and a part that is a responsible adult. Or you notice that a confident you emerges when you're with your close friends, while a self-conscious, shy you comes out around an intimidating stranger. In each situation, different parts of you are in charge, and it doesn't feel like you can do much about it. That's largely because you are not aware of the part that's in control at that moment.

There is actually an infinite number of other aspects of you. But just like a shattered mirror, when they are not recognized, they are out of synch with each other. This is a big reason it seems like we don't get what we want—we are only aware of what *certain* parts of ourselves want and are unaware of the desires of other parts.

So when the loving part of you wants to be in a close relationship but another part is afraid of being hurt, you have an internal conflict that plays itself out perfectly in your life. For all the lonely hearts out there, this is the true story.

Having a splintered consciousness doesn't mean you've done something wrong. It's just that some parts of you are stuck in places in the past where something frightening happened, or you didn't get your needs met, or you took on a negative belief that makes life seem difficult, and those parts haven't been able to move on. Unresolved trauma is a bad surprise that stays bad no matter how much time goes by. The child, teen, or adult that you were when it happened stays frozen in fear and helplessness, as if in a time capsule, and becomes a part of you that doesn't change or grow.

Because our brain is unable to deal with conflicting information unless it can be integrated, it tends to pick one perspective and repress all the information that doesn't fit. Then, as you experience more and more aspects of your life through that limited perspective, fear and helplessness can eventually become almost the only lens through which your brain chooses to see anything.

When you go inside yourself with the help of this book, you may sometimes discover the parts of you that are still frozen in the traumatic moment when you were hurt as a child, or hit by a car, or given a frightening medical diagnosis. But by revisiting these moments, you are seeing them with new eyes and bringing them into the present, so that part of you can be integrated with all the other various aspects of you.

If you simply notice the different outcomes in your life, and listen closely for the desires behind them, you will piece the mirror back together. The result is that the reflection slowly becomes harmonious.

For instance, when you begin to listen to your desire to stay home and play instead of dismissing it, you will find more opportunities to play—even at the office—and the child in you finally gets heard. In acknowledging both your confident part and your shy part, they are no longer cut off from each other, and so can begin sharing and merging their unique qualities.

Your consciousness will slowly become integrated and in less conflict with its parts. And the more that happens, the fewer surprises you'll have, because in the place of conflict you will discover certainty. As that begins to happen, you will begin to feel that you always get what you want. And it only happened when you decided to want it.

In what ways are you rigid? Go inside with that.
Are you rigid because of something you believe?
Go inside again.
What would happen if you didn't believe that?
What would this structure be like if it wasn't rigid?
Go in.

Rest easy.

"God" is a concept, and you can make God into anything you want. You can make it a Him, or a Her; you can make it angry or loving; you can make it approve or disapprove of anything you want; you can make it a part of any religion you like; you can even make it exist or not exist, because God is an idea.

This isn't to say there isn't meaning in God, for there is great meaning in what we look for in Him. We look for power, knowledge, judgment, punishment, salvation, heaven, hell . . . we look for as many things from Him as there are people to do the looking.

But the most important thing we look for is meaning. We look to Him to answer, "What is the meaning of life?" As long as you ask Him, you'll never find it because the premise is wrong. You aren't asking Him, you're asking *you.*

Realize this, and you will get your answer: The deepest meaning of life is that *you* give it meaning.

What does he know?
How does he feel?

You have probably heard the term *projection* used before, as in "You are projecting onto me" or "He is projecting onto her."

But what does *projection* really mean?

Projection is the story in your head that makes it *feel* like you're experiencing something or someone else. For instance, when you see a celebrity in a magazine or on TV and you think, "She has it all," or "He is so egotistical," that is a good example of projection. After all, you don't *know* these celebrities, yet you are certain they have those qualities.

Here is how it works:

In a movie theater, the story you see on the screen is not actually contained on the screen. The screen is blank. The story is in the projector's light, but you see it on the screen.

In the same way, when you're projecting, what you see is your story.

Remembering that you don't actually know those celebrities and yet feel sure that they have certain qualities is an easy way to discover this experientially. What this means is that you are the one who has it all; you are the one who is egotistical. You're just seeing those qualities in them. And the reason you don't know you're projecting is because you don't know yourself.

Though unrecognized projection keeps us from knowing ourselves by making it seem as if it is something or someone else we are experiencing, when you learn how to recognize projection at work it becomes an awesome tool for learning who you really are.

In order to do so, you just have to be able to catch yourself when you're doing it, and reel the projection back in.

For instance, if you find yourself thinking that your friend is jealous of you, and you start to feel her jealousy whenever something good happens to you, stop and reconsider. No matter how it seems, you don't actually experience anyone's thoughts or emotions but your own, so how could it be *her* jealousy that you feel? If you can simply acknowledge this, you can reel in the projection and discover that you might be the one who is jealous. If so, you can find out who or what you are jealous of, and why. Then, if you choose to, you can change it. When you were in the dark about your own jealousy, you had no power to choose. Now you do.

Likewise, if someone gives you a compliment and at first you refuse it, you can stop to consider that you might be projecting your own positive view of yourself onto someone else. When you reel in the projection you can accept this positive view and then experience the wonderful changes in how you feel about yourself that will result.

Another way of uncovering projection is when you have an argument with someone, and afterward you keep replaying it over and over in your mind. Since nobody else is there, you are actually arguing with yourself. And if this is true, then you've discovered an aspect of yourself that you previously didn't know about and that you are projecting onto someone else. You can reel it in by saying, *"Some part of me agrees with them but is denying it."* This will help you to realize that *the conflicts you have with others reflect the conflicts you have within yourself.*

The qualities that you don't know about are often the ones that block you from getting what you want. So in this case, instead of getting stuck on one side of an endless and exhausting argument, your awareness of the other side can help you to resolve the conflict more quickly.

When you do this you will begin to realize that anything anyone says to you is a message *from* you *to* you.

And this doesn't just apply to people you see, but with "the world" too.

For example, if you see cruelty in the world when you can close your eyes and let yourself feel it, you can know that it is actually your own cruelty—to yourself—that you see. Or when you see beauty and calm, you can remind yourself that it reflects your own harmony with yourself. Either way, you are discovering not just aspects of yourself, but entire realms that you did not previously know.

Taking these steps will not end projection all at once, but it will change the premise that you are seeing what's outside you into the premise that you are always experiencing yourself. If your unrecognized qualities are the source of the conflicts that block you from getting what you want, then the potential to change your life for the better by reeling in your projections is a prospect that is truly spellbinding.

As you start reeling in your projections—both the good and the bad—you will begin to understand that the universe is a great big mirror. What you see still looks like someone or something else, but you'll remember that it must be you. You experience what you *are*, and everything you see is a breadcrumb on the trail to the source of your being.

As you follow this path, you will discover your power. Anything anyone says is actually your own voice; anything anyone says to you is a message *from* you *to* you. When "*He* thinks" becomes "*I* think," you can begin to say no to certain things, and yes to others, and end the conflict altogether. You will have choices, where before you had none. And you will harness the power to change what seems to be outside of you by simply changing yourself.

Projection keeps you small. Recognition that you are what you see makes you big. And not because of anything you do, but because of what you *are*.

What is the person underneath the sheets expecting to see when he wakes up?

Close your eyes and see where that takes you.

What do you expect to see when you wake up every morning? Close your eyes and see where you go.

Imagine waking up every morning to a much better situation.

Every time you catch yourself expecting the old situation when you wake up, expect the new situation instead.

Be aware of what happens.

How many rainbows are there?

You probably answered one. But there are actually many rainbows.

There is one rainbow for each of the people on the observation deck; one for each person in the town who sees it; one for the photographer; one for the camera; one for you; and one for everyone who sees it in this book.

The reason the truth about the number of rainbows is so deceptive is that everybody who sees it generates an individual, virtual image of the rainbow that they "see" in their mind. This image is based on how our eyes and brain interpret the light; our memories of past rainbows, which we superimpose on this one; and humanity's collective decision to call this event a "rainbow."

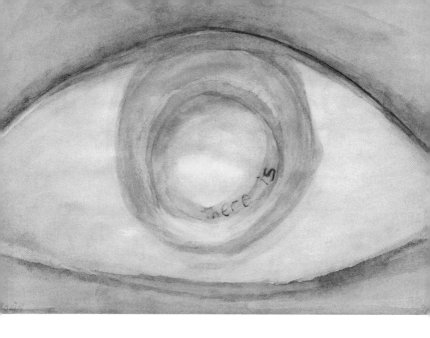

We don't really see what's there.

Our belief that we are seeing what is actually there comes from the incredible illusion of "sight" that our brain creates. Here's how it works:

Light enters through the iris and makes its way to the retina, which sends the information to the vision center of the brain. Using the information from these signals, the brain creates an impression of what is there—a table, your wife, a planet, a bee, anything. And this impression is based mostly on memories of what we were *taught* was there when we were children. So it is not your eyes that see, it is your brain that is interpreting what's there. And our brain mostly just lets us know what we already know, over and over again.

And the brain needs years of training to turn what the eyes

see into a meaningful image. That's because the brain cannot recognize what the eyes see without the training and the memory. This is why a young child cannot recognize a car, or a dog, or anything, for that matter, until they've been trained. Until then what a child sees is a field of information that only *becomes* a car after they've been told what it is and what to expect about it. This is also why people who lose their sight in early childhood and gain it back in adulthood still cannot see very much at all, since their brains were not trained to recognize anything.

In other words, we don't see much of what is *actually* there, we only see what we already think is there.

But it's nobody's fault. There is so much information around us that the brain has to filter out everything that is not crucial to our survival in order to keep us from being overwhelmed. But as we get older, we become less able to see anything that does not fit with what our memory tells us should be there. By that time we are seeing mostly memories.

Regardless of what we are actually seeing at any time, we are at all times surrounded by energy that is mostly invisible to us. Our vision center only "sees" what's there—such as a tree—if the atoms of the tree are vibrating at the same frequency as our vision center does. Just a little higher than that, and the tree would disappear or look like a ghost. Anything that vibrates higher or lower than our limited frequency range is completely invisible to us.

So what is actually there? Who can say?

What do you see?

Enter Here

Think about yesterday. What were you doing? How did you feel? Close your eyes. Notice what it looks and feels like. Pay attention to details. Let it come to life.

Now think about tomorrow. Where are you a day from now? How do you feel? What are you doing? Close your eyes and let it come to life.

Think of this infinity symbol as a time line. Find yesterday on it. Then, locate tomorrow on it.

If you can see and experience both times in the present, then is there a "past" and a "future," or are both happening right now? Go inside with that question.

Now, go inside and locate "now."

Anytime you find yourself thinking about the past or the future, visualize this symbol and find it there. Use the symbol as a reminder that you are making the past or the future now.

Time is an invention. When you close your eyes, you can experience any "time" you like, which means it's all happening now. And even the present isn't what it seems—the light from the sun you see now is actually eight minutes old. The images we get from space telescopes are from millions and even billions of years ago. The process of realizing that it's all happening now makes you less limited by time's restrictions and allows you to begin to sail above it altogether.

What is their condition?

Close your eyes and see what comes up.

Could there be information you don't have that would change the way you see them?

What would it be?

Close your eyes. Do you see them any differently?

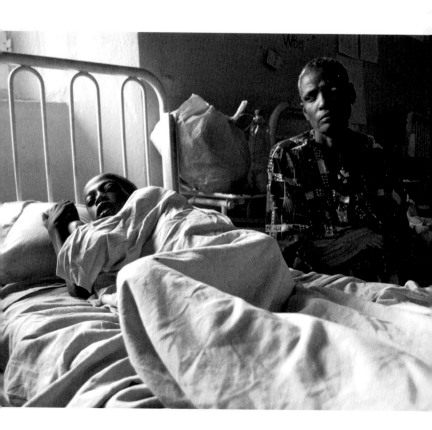

YES!

Have you ever felt left out of all the fun?

If you had to tell the story of every image you see in this book, you'd have to write another book the size of an encyclopedia for each one.

The reason you don't is because each image reflects a *part* of you that contains a *whole* experience. This concept is an essential part of what are called *holograms*.

What is a hologram?

Put simply, a hologram is a three-dimensional laser light image that has a totally realistic 3-D effect. The most famous hologram in history—the three-dimensional projection of a moving, speaking Princess Leia, emanating from R2-D2 in the film *Star Wars* as if she were really there—is a perfect example of what holograms in action look like.

But what is truly amazing about holograms is that every *part* of the holographic film contains and can reproduce the *whole* image. In other words, you could shatter a holographic image of a horse into many pieces and *you would still be able to see the entire horse in each fragment.*

The idea that each part of something contains the whole is not found just in holographic technology. You experience it in this book. But you also experience it in your life.

For instance, if you have ever smelled Play-Doh and suddenly the sights, the sounds, the smells, and the feelings of kindergarten came flooding back to life as if it were today, right now, then you are already familiar with a part of something containing the whole. In this case, the part—the scent of Play-Doh—contains the whole—the entire experience of kindergarten. The same goes if you have ever heard a song and been carried away to another time and place. The part, which is the song, contains the whole, which is the memory.

What this means is that very common, everyday experiences are in fact *holographic* in nature.

But the real wow-factor in this realization is that *you* are a part that contains the whole. The reason you can close your eyes and describe any person you know, see, or even imagine, is because they are holograms *contained within you*. In fact, the whole universe is instantly available to you, for contained within you are holograms of everything that exists in the cosmos. If you have ever felt small, consider that this means that you are as big as any cosmos you can see.

Understanding this means you can begin to see that holograms are actually all around us in our daily lives, and we experience them constantly. And recognizing them offers a powerful opportunity to learn how to get what you want more quickly and easily than you ever imagined.

One of the easiest ways to spot holograms is when they are *triggered*.

Pills are one of the more symbolic and easy-to-spot holographic triggers. When you take a headache pill, it is a trigger for a headache-free hologram to come. That is, the pill triggers a whole different experience, a different universe, a different pain-free you and everything that goes with it. This is why the mere thought of a remedy can make you feel better. Running into an old friend is a trigger that activates instant access to everything you know about them.

Suffice it to say that anything that alters your experience from one thing to another is a trigger—just think how the shift between yes and no can change everything—and that this alteration takes place in an instant and without the need for physical movement. And traveling without moving is called a *quantum leap*.

The funny thing about quantum leaps is that though they sound impossibly scientific or futuristic, as if they require technology only science fiction can currently muster, *we have them all the time*. Whether it is news that changes your entire world in an instant or words that change your mind forever, both are quantum leaps between holographic universes because you traveled from one existence to another without physically moving.

In other words, "Beam me up Scotty!" is something we already do.

The most significant gift an understanding of the holographic nature of the universe brings is greater freedom. When you see that the past and also the future are holograms—*your* holograms—it means you can change them. Just as the kindergarten you is still there after all these years and can be revisited instantly through the familiar scent of Play-Doh, any hologram of "you" can come to life in an instant when you need it, with nothing but a slight change in view. This is also why you can visualize winning a race before the actual race, for like the past, the future is a hologram you simply trigger with a thought.

That's because your brain itself works holographically. This is why, for example, you do not have to rewind back through every detail of the last ten years in order to remember something that happened ten years ago. Instead, the memory comes up instantaneously, along with all the sensory details of the time when it happened. It's all there and instantly accessible as soon as you look for it. That is because memories are holograms that you simply brush up against, not library books you pull off a shelf. Computers have *nothing* on your brain.

When you become aware of your holographic brain, and the holographic nature of reality and your existence in it, you will begin to harness its power. In doing so you will realize that *nothing* is far away. In fact, everything that is, was, or ever could be is a hologram that already exists here, and needs only to be triggered by you.

When we talk about igniting the genius within, that's what we mean.

What does this flag mean?

What is his plight?
Close your eyes.
Feel how he feels.
Give him voice.

What if the prison bars disappeared . . .
What does he do?
What happens to him?
Close your eyes and see what happens.

The reason we get trapped in situations and experiences that we would love to change is that we think the same thoughts over and over and over and over again.

The repetitious thought produces an experience that confirms the thought that produces the same experience again, ad infinitum.

The result is a feedback loop in our lives that makes it very hard to change, because, as with all feedback loops, you can't find where it starts or ends.

This induces the powerlessness so familiar to the human experience.

Here's how it goes:

The reason you're poor is because you think you're poor.

Thinking it makes you feel poor.

Feeling it makes you act poor.

Acting it makes you become poor.

Becoming it confirms that you are poor.

Then you think you're poor.

And on and on and on.

It all starts with a thought.

But there is a way out.

First, stop thinking it.

Stop saying it to yourself or to anyone else.

Because whenever you think it or say it, you're making it, so just clear your plate.

Then, start thinking and saying the new thought, such as "I have plenty of money," or "I will have plenty of money"—whatever feels believable to you.

Start focusing on the money you *do* have.

Then you will begin to see opportunities for more money, because now you're *looking* for it.

Every time anything related to money comes up, repeat the new thought.

First you'll notice that you've stopped feeling poor, and you've started feeling like you have enough.

And it feels good.

Then you begin to expect money—or love, or joy, or trust, kindness, confidence, faith, partnership, knowledge, abundance, clarity, peace, or anything else you've longed for—just like you used to expect poverty.

And that feels good.

Continue to concentrate on having these things as much as you concentrated on *not* having them, and notice the difference in your world.

The only reason we aren't aware of this
is because we think something totally different.

Think of a powerful memory from your past. It could be any kind of memory—good or bad, happy or sad—whatever comes up. Close your eyes and revisit it. Notice what you see and feel.

Now imagine putting yourself, as an adult, into the memory so that there are two of you—the past you and the current you—together.

You can watch, encourage, talk to, rescue, teach, impart knowledge or wisdom . . . do whatever you really wish you could do. Nothing is impossible. Close your eyes and see what happens.

Sometime in the next few days close your eyes and revisit the memory again. Notice what it looks and feels like now.

All is forgiven.

This is a cancer cell.

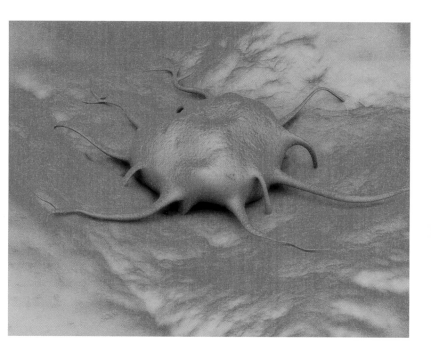

What is it doing?

Where does it come from?

What is its story?

Go in.

**See if you can locate where a thought,
any thought, comes from.
Close your eyes and try.**

Then close your eyes and try to locate the place from which you decided to close your eyes.

You might even try to locate the place from which your desire to open to this page originated.

If you couldn't do it, don't worry, because thoughts and desires don't come from a *place*. They come from a field of pure possibility. Your intention to think a certain thought, move an arm, sing a certain note—you name the desire—gives the possibility a form. Until then it doesn't exist.

What's in the black box?
Close your eyes, picture it, and see what comes up.
By deciding what's in it,
you have created the thing you decided upon,
out of an infinite number of possible things.
Close your eyes and open the box.

Close your eyes and think of an apple.

Did it exist before you thought of it? Did it stop existing after?

　　Where did it come from? Where did it go? Close your eyes and see where that takes you.

Next time you eat an apple, ask yourself the same questions.

In our thoughts and our dreams we accept that whatever we imagine simply appears when we give thought to it, and disappears when we stop. But in our waking, physical lives we assign a story to everything we see—about where it came from and where it went.

We don't really know where anything came from. Before we see it, it did not exist for us. After we no longer see it, it disappears. We can imagine or believe a story about where it came from and went, but that is nothing but a thought too.

Do you think you know everything there is to know?

Go inside.

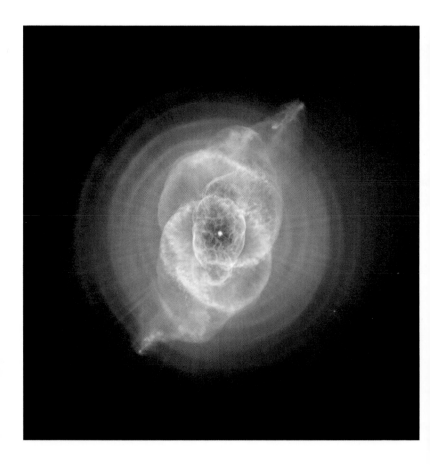

Enjoy being.

Is this love?

When you look at this image,
what do you feel?

Have you ever been drawn to anything?

Have you ever been irresistibly attracted to a person, a place, a food, a kind of music, a color, a sport, a dance, an animal, or a career, anything at all, so much that when faced with it you can't concentrate on anything else?

We tend to think of this powerful feeling as something unique and rare . . . so rare, in fact, that we're lucky if we ever feel it at all.

But attraction is not rare—we're surrounded by it.

The reason we don't see it is because we have taught ourselves to see a mechanized universe, rather than a feeling one; a universe that operates through randomness or laws rather than love and attraction. The result is that we feel deprived of the incredible passion, meaning, fascination, well-being, vitality, sexual energy, and creativity that come from simple attraction . . . in other words, everything that makes us feel alive.

And yet we are not actually deprived, for we are not just surrounded by attraction, we are swimming in it.

Like sunflowers that follow the sun all day long, love-struck by the light, plants turn toward the sun not just because they need it, but because they are *attracted* to it. You can see the same force of attraction at work when a squirrel runs to a tree; a lion runs after its prey; a planet circles its sun; or galaxies hurtle toward one another through space at incomprehensible speeds, inexorably headed for a cosmic embrace that will last billions of years.

In short, you can see attraction at work anytime one thing moves toward another.

And attraction doesn't just occur in nature. You can observe an abundance of attraction in your own life.

Whenever you feel a tug in your heart to go somewhere; when what you need comes right to you without any effort—the way your life fills up with people who are *exactly* where you are now; when you begin to work on something and opportunities begin to come your way; anytime you are taught something you didn't know and then begin to see it everywhere; when you have the same experiences over and over; or when you recognize the cosmic precision of an unbelievable coincidence, you are experiencing the power of attraction at work. Look around you at what is there now and realize that whomever or whatever you see is there as a result of a mutual, and undeniable, attraction.

As you begin to see attraction operating, your awareness of it will eventually expand to encompass the understanding that attraction isn't just bountiful, it's universal. It determines every aspect of our lives and life itself. Without it the atoms in your body would fly apart; the Earth would disintegrate; the stars would disassemble; and the universe itself would unravel into absolute nothingness. When you look at it this way, you can see that attraction isn't just universal, it's what brings the universe to life.

The deepest wisdom to be gained from the understanding of attraction's powerful role in our lives is the discovery of attraction's source, which is love. Look deep in your heart anytime you feel attracted to anything or anyone, and you will find love there. It may require a little digging—we've become so afraid to feel our love that we often feel its pull but without the joy, making it hard to recognize. But next time you hear irresistibly beautiful music, if you stop and listen closely, you will know then that the source of attraction is love.

When you do, you will come to the greatest realization of all—that all forms of attraction, including gravity itself, are expressions of love. Therefore the universe is held together not just by attraction, but by love.

To go from living in a mechanical universe to a loving universe requires what is called a *quantum leap* to get there, which is a voyage that does not require physical travel. And quantum leaps don't get much bigger than that.

So ultimately attraction is not something you have to believe in, but rather it's something you can see with your own eyes. And once you know your own power of attraction better, you will know its source. When you do, you will not only begin to see and feel love everywhere and in everything, you will begin to feel *in love* with the universe . . . and that it is in love with you.

Where does "the news" come from? Close your eyes and answer the question.

What if the news was always *positive, good news*? Close your eyes and see where you go.

If you heard more good news, how would that change things for you? How would you feel? What would the world look like?

Go inside and contemplate.

What is he so happy about?

The brain is the only part of the body that cannot move on its own.

Yet not only does it create physical movement in our bodies by simple visualization, it can go anywhere it likes to go, even to the far reaches of the universe, by using the same power. This is why you can travel to anywhere in any time just by imagining it, and why you can experience anything at all when you are dreaming.

So the brain is both immobile and boundless at the same time. This ability to travel without moving is called a *quantum leap.* And if your brain does it, *you* do it.

Go inside and don't think about pink elephants.

What happens?

What does this tell you?

Where is the Internet?

Where is the business world?

Where is the fashion world?

Where is the political world?

Where is "the News"?

Where is the gay world?

Where is "the military"?

Where is "the world of sports"?

Go inside and see if you can find them.

Does he feel loss?
Go inside, picture him, and answer the question.

Do you feel loss? If so, what have you lost?
Go inside and see what comes up.

Does he see what you've lost?
Go inside and see where that takes you.

What are you hungry for?

Think about something or someone who came into your life so easily that you didn't even have to try. Go inside.

See if you can think of other times this has happened. Notice how it felt. Close your eyes and see what comes up.

Next time something comes easily, make note of it.

Right now, you are traveling at mind-boggling speeds.

You are on the Earth, which rotates on its axis at 1,070 miles an hour.

The Earth is traveling 67,000 miles an hour around the sun.

Along with our solar system, the Earth is traveling 486,000 miles an hour around the center of the Milky Way galaxy.

And with your galaxy you are traveling at massive speeds through intergalactic space . . .

. . . all without any effort, or awareness, on your part.

Go inside with this.

You take all kinds of things for granted—that you travel at astonishing speeds; that the sun will rise; that there is air to breathe. And the greatest thing you take for granted is that you came into existence, which required no effort on your part at all. But taking things for granted is not a bad thing. It is a window into the effortlessness that abounds in your life and in the universe.

What kind of relationship do they have?
Tell their story.

Close your eyes and see if you can think of a story in your life that makes you unhappy, such as "I never have enough time," "I'll never get paid what I'm worth," "I'm aging," "My partner doesn't respect me," "The world is going to pot," "People can't be trusted," whatever comes to mind.

Now visualize a chalkboard with the story written on it.

Imagine erasing it. What happens? Do you notice any changes in your body? Close your eyes and see what unfolds.

Look for changes in what you see and how you feel.

The next time you hear this story in your mind or see it playing out in your life, try simply erasing it. You might even try writing a new, better story on the chalkboard. See what happens.

This chick took his first flight three days after this photograph was taken.

How did he know it was time?

What if you lived your life, twenty-four hours a day, as if it were a dream?

Look around you right now and imagine that, in spite of how it feels, you are actually dreaming.

Go inside.

See yourself walking down a familiar street, knowing that you are in a dream. What do you see ahead of you on the horizon? How is it materializing as you move forward?

What would you like to have happen in your dream?

Close your eyes and make it happen.

If your life were actually a dream, how would that change things? Close your eyes and see where you go.

We are taught to believe that waking life is real, and dreams are not.

But your waking life and your dream life have one powerful thing in common: Your mind creates both of them.

In your sleeping dreams there are gradations of awareness. First is the most common state—total unconsciousness—in which you are not aware that it's a dream, so it seems like the dream is happening to you. The next step up is some awareness that it's a dream, so you have some control—like when you try to wake up from a nightmare because you've realized you're dreaming. The highest state of dream consciousness is called lucid dreaming, in which you are acutely aware that you are dreaming, and you have a lot of control over what happens. If you've ever found yourself directing your dream as it happens, then you are onto what we are talking about.

The waking-dream state that you are probably in right now, if you are listening to the soundtrack, is somewhere in between. In this unique dream state, similar to a daydream, you can choose either to control the outcome of the dream, or let it unfold as it would when you're asleep. But in both cases, you are still awake.

We have more power in our dreams because we acknowledge that they are exclusively an internal experience that we create in our minds. This frees us up to do exactly as we feel without limitation. In our dreams we solve impossible math equations, invent brilliant new products, compose beautiful music. In our dreams, we fly. We don't consider our dreams to be real because they don't obey the rules: Time and space have no bounds, so there is limitless potential, and complete freedom. Therefore they *can't* be real.

We believe that waking life is mostly an external experience that is happening to us, so we perceive that we have very limited power when we're awake. This perception ties us to rules that not only limit our possibilities but bind our very spirit.

However, since your dreams and your waking life have the same source—your mind—then one might be just as real as the other. That would mean that the same gradations of awareness you have in your dreams would also apply in your waking life. The only way to find out if that's true is to remove the limitations and rules you abide by in your waking life to make room for the kind of endless possibility you experience in your dream life.

If you do so, you might just find that your waking life and your dream life have something else in common: Both are dreams, and both are real.

This is your Cosmic Profile.

As with an Internet profile where you can upload pictures and information about yourself that show you are a certain kind of person, you can use the Cosmic Profile to upload any version of yourself you'd like, without limitation.

You can upload a happy you; a healthy you; a successful you; a beautiful you; a freer you; a you with a particular outcome, you name it. With one touch of the button the whole story of the "you" you create uploads into the universe.

So imagine any you you want. Then, press the button, close your eyes, and watch not just the you, but the whole story around it, upload. Look for changes.

> **Note:** You can go back anytime and upload anything you like—an outcome, a feeling, a thing . . . a whole universe if you like.

What qualities does this night sky possess?

Close your eyes, call up the image, and let yourself become aware of its qualities.

See where that takes you.

When you look up at the night sky in an area unobstructed by city lights—such as in this photo taken in a Dark Sky park in the Arizona desert—you have the opportunity to lose yourself in the infinite vastness of what we call the Milky Way galaxy. But even in a literal sense, you are as vast as the infinite universe. Your brain has more potential connections than there are stars in the visible universe, which has been estimated at 70 sextillion, or 70,000,000,000,000,000,000,000. So your single brain alone is on par with the most incomprehensibly wondrous starry night you could ever contemplate.

Close your eyes and think of something that would deeply offend, upset, or anger you if someone said it in front of you or to you.

Now, close your eyes again.

Who is saying it?

Since the person isn't saying it now, who is actually saying it?

Close your eyes and see where that takes you.

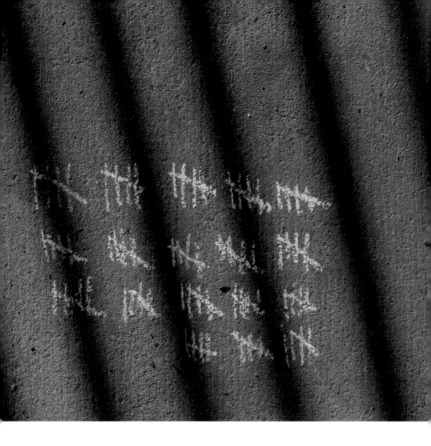

Who made these marks, and why?
Close your eyes and answer the question.

Can you imagine erasing the marks?
How does that feel?

Have you felt like that before?
Close your eyes and see if you can remember.

Do you ever imagine yourself performing your favorite song, making a winning touchdown, or giving an acceptance speech? Do you ever imagine being uncharacteristically assertive, fearless, or successful? Who is this person you imagine? Can you describe him? How does he or she feel? Close your eyes and explore their personality.

Close your eyes again. Imagine looking in a mirror, seeing yourself, and touching one hand to the glass so that you join hands with the mirror image. As you're looking at yourself, let your reflection in the mirror gradually morph into the person you imagine. Take notice of every detail you see.

With your hand still on the mirror, let yourself become the person you see so that you and your reflection match on both sides of the mirror. How do you feel now? What do you want to do? Imagine that.

Next time you need this aspect of yourself, use the mirror to call her or him up.

Is he thinking right now?

If not, how does he do it?

When you think of a wave, you think of water that is spread out and in motion.

But water is not the only thing that exists in a wave-like form. What quantum physics has revealed is that *everything* is a wave.

You've probably heard of quantum physics, but it might not mean anything to you. You gather that scientists are doing something in a laboratory, but you'll never understand it. And why would you? You don't live in a laboratory.

But you do live in a laboratory, and this laboratory is called your life.

Scientists look for the smallest things they can find, and they call those things particles. What quantum physicists were shocked to discover is that every particle is actually a wave spread out everywhere . . . until it gets looked for. Only when a researcher tries to find it does the wave then turn into a particle, which scientists call "collapsing" the wave. As a wave it has infinite possibilities for where it can be and what it can do. But as a particle it has been converted into just one thing located in just one place. In other words, the really tiny stuff that makes up physical reality is both infinitely everywhere in the form of a wave of possibility that can be turned into anything, and right here right now in the form of a specific thing we can see. This means that there are, quite literally, infinite possibilities, and the observer (that's you) determines which one appears.

So the conclusion of a hundred years of quantum physics is that you get exactly what you're looking for.

Because every person is an observer, and we and the physicists live in the same universe, each of us has the same power to affect the "quantum field"—which is to say your life—through observation and choice. And you are already doing it—it's just that you do it mostly unconsciously. But whether you realize it or not, you never cease to "collapse" possibilities into outcomes. Even deciding to go to the grocery store instead of staying in to do laundry is collapsing waves of possibility into particles of outcomes. You can't escape it.

The revelation and power comes when you realize that you are doing it, so that you can begin to select possibilities more consciously by witnessing them in your mind, and then waiting for them to appear in your life. That is the point of this book—to help you begin to select your possibilities with greater awareness and fewer limits.

It goes even deeper, because consider this: If a particle is in an infinite number of places at once in its wave state, then on some level so are we. We don't usually feel that in our waking life, but we certainly surf the waves of possibility when we're dreaming. The soundtrack you're listening to is helping you to ride the waves right now.

Everything in the universe, including you, is made up of waves and particles. This means that you yourself are part of literally infinite possibilities. In some sense, there are no limits to where you can go, and who you can become, because every possibility for yourself that you can conceive of already exists . . . and experiencing any particular one is just a matter of riding that wave.

Hidden in this picture is a portrait of a young woman and an old woman. Look at the image and allow yourself to discover the two portraits. But don't look too hard. Let your eyes relax, don't focus, and wait for the two distinct figures to appear to you. Once you discover the two distinct portraits, close your eyes and see where you go.

Close your eyes and think of an issue in your life that you are sure you can only look at one way. For example, "I can never get out of this relationship," or "I can never do any other kind of work," whatever occurs to you.

Look at the picture until you can go back and forth between the two realities embedded within the single portrait. Then close your eyes and think of your issue again. Is there more to see this time?

Assuming that there is only one portrait does not mean there is only one, but it does mean that you only see one. Your life is no different. Assuming that what you see is all that's there does not mean it is all that's there . . . it just means that's all you see.

Have you ever found money in a jacket, a book, or an account that you didn't know you had? Have you ever had money come to you from out of nowhere, like an unexpected check or gift? Go inside and relive it.

If you had known that money was coming, what would you have done differently? How would you have seen things? Go inside and replay it with that new knowledge.

Could it be that right now you have more money than you realize? If so, would you see or do things differently? Go inside with that.

A wormhole is a shortcut through space and time.

It is a portal through which you can travel vast distances almost instantaneously. The moment you move into a wormhole, you're already there.

But wormholes aren't just something out in "space"—they exist here. They are shortcuts for getting you from one place to another place you want to go. For example, right now think about something you want that is far off or seems hard to do. What could happen that would make it much closer or easier? Like meeting the right person, receiving vital information, or stumbling onto something helpful—whatever occurs to you. Consider that it could *actually* happen. Then start paying attention to any opportunity that comes your way . . . and take note when it does, because you've found a wormhole.

Wormholes are everywhere. You only need to recognize them in order to instantly travel through them.

Let's say that you are waiting on a subway platform late at night after a hard day at work. You are there to meet and walk your wife home, but she's very late, and you're getting hot, tired, and really irritated. Finally you see her walking toward you. *You have a choice.* Instead of looking and sounding angry, you decide to smile and express the joy you actually feel upon seeing her. She in turn beams lovingly back at you, and the rest of the evening goes wonderfully.

You just chose a wormhole. It was an instant shortcut to a better outcome.

Once you know what a wormhole is, you can spot one quite easily, and then you only have to choose to travel through it. A wormhole can be anything that opens up passage to a different *story* than the one you already know. Focusing your attention on every loving gesture, instead of experiencing your partner as neglectful; looking at a picture in a magazine that gives you a really good feeling; getting flowers; eating ice cream—all are potential wormholes because they change the way you're feeling instantly, and you're already *there* experiencing it the moment it happens.

By the way, cell phones, television, and e-mails are also wormholes, as are the images in this book. All are shortcuts that carry you to someplace in the past, present, or future, but you do not require time or travel to get there.

The trick is to recognize how wormholes can help you, *and decide to use them.*

You're already there.

To be spiritual or to become enlightened is not about being anything other than what you are.

The idea that you have to change to do either—that you have to not love what you love, to edit how you truly feel, to believe that what you are at this moment is somehow not right—stems from the notion that only certain things are "spiritual," while others are not. With this premise, in order to become spiritual you must reject everything in yourself that does not measure up.

This approach to spirituality does not make you more spiritual. Instead, it produces conflict between how you actually feel and how you *allow* yourself to feel. And the result of this conflict is shame.

Though it is rarely recognized, this sense of shame over who you are creates a natural fear of and resistance to enlightenment, because it conflicts with the human spirit's great passion to be *real.*

What is real? Being real is accepting what any part of you actually feels right now. It is simply recovering your innate acceptance of yourself that you had at birth, but which you lost as you began to learn what was wrong with you.

Being real isn't the same as being nice, or moral, or unselfish, or spiritual, or even safe. Being real can be disruptive only because we have constructed lives based mostly on how we are *supposed* to feel, instead of how we actually feel. After all, if you are a spiritual person and you find that you are angry or that you love something you're not supposed to, you may find it problematic to express your anger or your love because of the conflict you'll experience between having that emotion and the idea that it is not spiritual to do so.

If you don't know what real is anymore, then imagine what you would do if there were no consequences of any kind, and you'll find it there. You can also find your realness by recognizing the conflict that arises when you attempt to repress who you are. Behind this conflict you will find the hidden shame. Bring love and acceptance there and you will bring your real self out into the light where it belongs, and you will discover what real enlightenment is all about.

While being real often doesn't appear very spiritual, it is profoundly healing. If you simply allow yourself to be angry, you will no longer be resisting how you truly feel. This puts an end to the conflict within you. And when you are no longer in conflict with yourself, you will no longer be angry. Just by allowing yourself to be angry, you stop being angry. This may also have a powerful effect on those around you, which changes your story (and theirs). So being real *is* enlightened because in *accepting* how you feel, you replace shame with love.

And when you go down the path of being real rather than "spiritual"—to get out of your own way and just let yourself *be*—you will begin to see the truth, which is that you are *already* spiritual. You can't help but be. After all, if your spirit's defining characteristic is its intangibility—its lack of physicality—then you can observe that everything that is truly, definitively you is already nonphysical. Your emotions, your thoughts, your dreams, your imagination, your creativity, your ideas, the movie screen of your mind upon which you witness any reality you can possibly conceive, are all nonphysical in nature. And yet they define your experience. They are here, and yet not here, which means this is the case for you too.

So you couldn't be more spiritual if you tried.

Think of someone you feel sorry for. Close your eyes and see where you go.

Why do you feel sorry for them?
    Close your eyes again and see where that takes you.

There is no power in your life greater than your own. We fear this possibility because we think that if we embrace it, then we are to blame for what has gone wrong in our lives. But if you let go of blame altogether, the premise turns into one of unlimited power—that you have the potential to make every good thing you've ever wanted for yourself come true. Because, in fact, it isn't just that there is no power in your life greater than your own—there is no power in your life *other* than your own.

To realize that you are the source of all that you know, all that you see, and all that you experience is not narcissistic, egoistical, or sacrilegious. It is accepting who you are. Labeling it a boastful act of the ego not only distorts the infinite creative power you possess, it also forever keeps you from grasping it. The number-one way you can show reverence and gratitude is to accept this gift, and use it.

**When you are with another person,
it is not the other person you experience.**
It is always you that you experience with any
person . . . your feelings, your thoughts,
your expectations, everything.

The "other person" you experience is an
image in your mind of the person, which you
imbue with your own thoughts, feelings, and
expectations that come up when you are
with that person,
or when you simply think of them.

This photograph from the Antarctic shows water in all three of its states: liquid, gas, and frozen. Though water is always water, it expresses itself in different ways. So sometimes it flows, sometimes it mists, and sometimes it is solid.

People are just like water—they are always people, but they have different states of being and express themselves in different ways. (In fact the human body is made up mostly of water.)

With this in mind, when do you flow? When do you mist? When are you solid?

Close your eyes and see where you go.

When you're dreaming,
with your eyes closed in a dark room,
where does your brain get the light
to "see" your dream?

The light must come from some inner
energy source.

What if it comes from the energy of the
starry universe within you?

How did this person manage to fly?
Have you ever done something like this yourself?
Close your eyes and see what comes up.

When was the last time you had an "evil" thought?

What was it?

Go inside and play it out in your mind. Don't hold back.

Is there something you feel *blocked* about—like you just can't move forward? Close your eyes and see what comes up. Focus on how it *feels*.

The deepest recesses of our selves are mute. They do not speak using words, conceptualize what's happening, or try to reason their way through life. Instead they operate on instinct, reflexes, and ancient survival mechanisms. In other words, these parts of us just are, without any idea about it. But they do communicate with us all the time through our dreams that exist without language, and our feelings and body sensations, which speak for themselves. When we don't understand these messages—when we are confounded by our feelings and confused by our dreams—we tend to experience it as a block that is holding us back. But in fact the answer is embedded within the block itself. In other words, the block is the message. So next time you feel hindered in some way that you can't explain, don't try to. Just let it be. And give yourself enough time and space to let the answer come to you.

What do you consider to be impossible?

Go in.

**Next time you feel bored, old,
or that you've seen it all, try this:**

Really look at something you've looked at many times. For instance, pick a house or a building in your neighborhood that you've passed by countless times and really *look* at it as if you've never seen it before.

If you do this enough you will be quite surprised to find that there are buildings in your neighborhood that you've never seen before. You can do this with anything or anyone. And the more you do it the more you will see . . . and the more you will be surprised.

There is so much information *around us* that the brain has to filter out everything that is not crucial to our survival in order to be able to see what is. The problem arises as we get older and begin to *only* see memories, so that it becomes really difficult to see anything new. This is sometimes why people get stuck in the past, and why life becomes boring or stale. But the ability to train yourself to see new things never goes away, which means you can become like a child again just with the power of sight.

Close your eyes and imagine yourself flipping channels, tuning in the channel of your choice.

Close your eyes and do it again, only this time imagine every channel playing a different outcome for your life . . . one channel where, for instance, you travel to a place you always wanted to visit; another where you never get to go there; one channel where you have enough money to buy a house; another where you can only afford to rent an apartment . . . whatever comes to mind.

Think of a situation you don't like.

Then switch channels in your mind to an outcome that you do like.

Every time you find yourself expecting a situation you don't like,

Switch channels to a situation you do like.

Watch for changes.

141

What does she see?

We normally think of a mirror as a reflective surface in which we see ourselves. But conventional mirrors do not actually do this because they only show your body.

For a mirror to reflect you, it has to do more than reflect your body. Instead, it has to reflect something much more significant: your *being*. In order to see all of who you are, your definition of a mirror has to change.

What is your being?

Unlike your body, your being is not something you can physically locate. Nevertheless your being is everything about you that truly determines your experience, like your thoughts, your emotions, your beliefs, your desires, your past, and your future. Your being also includes aspects of you which you may have never thought of as *you* at all, such as people, places, and things you can see.

So you can define your being as literally anything you see, know, feel, or think of. Rather than representing any part of your experience, your being is the whole of it. You can think of your being as the totality of you.

The point is to use this book as a way to begin to find out who . . . and what . . . you really are.

Imagine yourself as a child, and go into this scene.
As a child, what would you do with this space?
Close your eyes, and do whatever you want to do.

What does the child look like and feel like?
Close your eyes and get to know this child.

As the adult you are now, join the child in this scene
(so both your adult self and your child self are together).
What does the child see that is different from what you see?
Is there anything you want to say to the child?
Close your eyes and spend some time together.

Later, drift back and review all the things you imagined.
What did you discover?

Go in.

Look closely at any item that is near you.
Now close your eyes and picture that same item in your mind.

Where is the screen of the mind upon which you see the image?

Ask yourself that question and go inside.

Think about a problem you have. Contemplate it.

Now, describe the color orange . . .
without using references to known orange-colored objects.
No matter how hard it gets, don't give up.

When you get to the point where you feel you are going to lose
your mind, quickly close your eyes. Go back to the problem. This
time, don't "think" about it. In fact, don't do anything. Just notice
where you go.

Think about a recent coincidence that seemed odd, such as a time you thought about someone you hadn't seen in years and then you ran into them the very next day; a time when much-needed help for an urgent problem seemed to come out of nowhere; a time you applied for a job the very moment they needed someone; whatever comes to mind. Those "impossible coincidences" are called synchronicities.

Go in and relive your synchronicity.

How did it feel?
Did it relate to anything else going on in your life?
Go inside with that.

Next time you have a synchronicity, take note.

Where is paradise?
Go inside and see what comes up.

We have taught ourselves that "paradise" or "heaven" is somewhere far from here. But any recollection of moments of happiness, elation, joy, bliss, or contentedness reveals the truth—that our emotions determine what we see and how things look, not where we are. If you've ever been depressed on a beautiful day or delighted on a rainy day, then you know that how we feel determines whether we're in heaven, hell, or somewhere in between. The truth embedded in these common experiences is that paradise is a thought, not a place. So if you want to figure out how to make it to heaven, the trick is to realize that you're already there.

What we know of "the world"—whether it is countries, economies, religions, wars, politics, or the environment, all of it—is seen through the prism of one central idea, that of *not enough* . . .

. . . not enough land, not enough nature, not enough money, not enough resources, not enough power, not enough God, not enough time. The reason we see this prevailing condition in the press and with our own eyes is not because the world doesn't have enough. Rather, it is our own personal sense of lack that we project onto the world. The world, both our concept of it and the actual planet, is simply reflecting back that projection. In other words, it is not "the world" that we see. It is ourselves.

So the reason we feel there isn't enough doesn't actually stem from a lack of resources. We feel there isn't enough because we've lost access to and awareness of all our parts, which we can see and feel everywhere but do not claim as our own. Somewhere along the way we have all lost ourselves, and as a result we feel finite when we are actually infinite. And the world reflects it.

One way out of the seemingly impossible problems the world suffers from is to realize that what you think of as the world and all its parts is actually you. If you do this, you can help recover your own sense that you are as big as the world that you see. And both you and the world are exactly as abundant as you feel.

When we each individually begin to recognize our limitless nature, connect to the parts of us we've been denying, and allow ourselves to *be* it all, we will start to see a different picture: the awesome, astonishing beauty and abundance in the world. As we raise our conscious awareness of our own power, this can become our future.

There will finally be enough.

This is a picture of your future.
You can fill it in with anything you like—any outcome,
any state of being, any kind of life you'd like to have,
any feeling at all.
What do you see?

Think of something you feel you don't have enough of.

Then take in this image for as long as you like.

Close your eyes and see where you go.

Think of a time you learned a new detail about a situation and the information dramatically changed your understanding of everything that had happened before.

Examples might be a time a close friend confessed they were much older than they had told you; someone you did not know was gay came out of the closet; or a time you walked into a surprise party and then you found out how everybody had kept the secret from you.

Go inside and see if you can recall an event where new information changed your understanding of what happened before.

Whenever something like this happens, the whole back-story changes. You revisit all the events that came before, but now nothing looks the same. The past comes alive, and you see it in a different light because of what you've learned. In other words, *the past changes.*

With this concept in mind, look at the image. Then go inside and see where it takes you.

Your mind is like a time machine that travels without moving. Not only can it experience the past and the future at any time, it can also change it. So time travel is something we already do. We just don't realize it.

Relax.

These pills will cure anything.

Close your eyes and take one.

What happens?

We are all terrorists.

And not just that. We're all thieves, murderers, bullies, rapists, pedophiles, slave traders, torturers, warmongers, you name it. It may seem like all the "bad guys" are out in the world attacking us from every corner, but they're only out there because we refuse to see that they're in us. If right now you are saying you could never do any of those things, think about how incredibly cruel you can sometimes be to yourself; so if you close your eyes and see a terrorist, a torturer, or a warmonger, know that you are one.

The power in this is discovering that the real enemy isn't out there in the form of a bogeyman out to get us. It's inside us. But it isn't our inner terrorist that's the problem . . .

The real enemy is shame.

Since the beginning of human history, we have told ourselves that we are inherently and dangerously evil, and that we must reject our "bad" qualities and feel ashamed when we discover them. So we try to hide all evidence of our imperfection, while mercilessly judging and tormenting ourselves about any quality that makes us uncomfortable.

The result of all this hiding is that we do not know ourselves. And because of this huge gap in our understanding of who we are, there is more terrorism, more murder, more war, more torture, and more pedophilia, than we could ever have imagined.

The lesson is that shame does not heal us. Instead, it robs us of choice.

Expressing every single aspect of ourselves is only a problem when it's not a choice. If you can't control it—if it just happens—it's a compulsion. So you're not *choosing* to be enraged if you can't also choose to be calm. And you're not really choosing to be "good," either, if you can't also choose not to be good . . . and being compulsively nice, kind, and perfect, but not real, is just a different way of being cruel to yourself by covering up feelings you're ashamed of.

The reason there is so much terrorism and so much war is because we have robbed ourselves of choice.

This counts for the "bad guys" too. Bullies feel more helpless than their victims, but can't bear to know it. Terrorists have lost touch with their own feelings of vulnerability and compassion, so they have no choice but to expend their life energy strategizing how to best strike fear into the hearts of others. You're not really choosing to be rigid, relentless, and cruel if you can't also choose to be trusting and open.

Shame robs us of our creative energy and cripples our infinite capacity to feel and be everything that we are. As a result we are bereft of the missing parts of ourselves, including the "bad" and the "vulnerable" parts. And we are exhausted by not letting ourselves simply be real.

But if we choose to accept that we are all the horrible characters we see on the world stage, it means that we accept them on our internal stage. In so doing, we will no longer need to act that conflict out on the world. In other words, accept that you are a terrorist, and you will find that you have a choice to be a terrorist or not. When choice enters the picture, "terrorism" can end.

Having reclaimed every aspect of ourselves, we reclaim our power to choose every minute how we want to be, which is what real creativity is all about.

What do you believe about rattlesnakes?
Go inside and see what comes up.

What if you believed something different?
Close your eyes and see what happens.

Close your eyes and create a new belief about something in
your life, such as "Things always go my way," or "I always have
enough." Whatever you like.

Notice any changes.

When you change the way you look at something,
you change the very thing you're looking at.

The answer you seek in life is not found in what you *have* to do, but in what you *love* to do.

Follow this path and you will experience astounding changes.

Doing, getting, and being what you love is your greatest contribution to an enlightened world. Rejecting what is here and what we really love has done nothing for humanity but bring suffering beyond measure.

Allow yourself to do, to get, and to be what you love, and you will realize that you are not here on Earth just to learn or to heal so you can get back to the "spiritual realm." In other words, you didn't come "here" just to get back "there." However, by allowing yourself to do what you love, you will finally begin to do what you are really here to do, which is to *live*.

No individual bee in this photo is "intelligent." Each bee has one job to do, but none have any idea what the goal of the swarm is. There is no leader giving instructions to the individual bees. And yet the group achieves a larger goal that no individual bee is aware of.

So while no individual bee is intelligent, the swarm has an intelligence of its own.

If no single bee knows what the goal is, who or what does? Go inside with that.

Have you ever been involved in a group that created something greater than what the individuals in it intended? Go inside.

Think of a time something extraordinary, impossible, or amazing happened.

How did it feel? Close your eyes and recall the event.

How did things look before the event? What about after? Go in and see what comes up.

Could it be something extraordinary will happen again? Close your eyes and see where you go.

I was thinking about thinking.

And then I started to think, maybe I shouldn't think so much?

Or maybe I should just *let* myself think.

So I thought about that.

Is this creativity?

What is love?

Where is it?

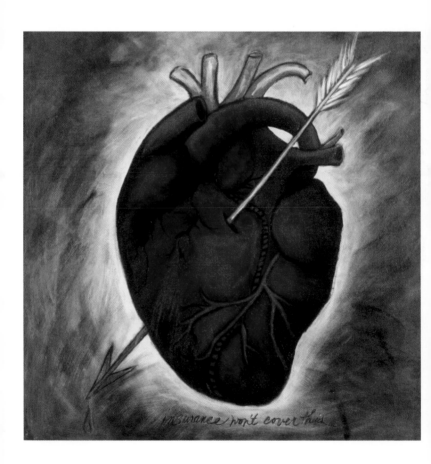

Which came first, the chicken or the egg?

The answer is neither. The reason you can't see this—the reason we're flummoxed by this question—is not because it's a paradox that can't be solved.

It's because the *premise* of the question is wrong. In order to see this you have to take a step back and see the question from a greater perspective.

When you do you'll find the answer is in fact obvious: Neither the chicken *nor* the egg came first. You did. That's why you can make the chicken first, you can make the egg first, or you can make them both first. You can make *anything* first because *you* came first.

When you catch on to this secret—that the premise determines what you see, and that a false premise can keep you from finding the answer—you will discover that all of the questions and related insurmountable problems, paradoxes, and traps that the world faces are in fact answerable and solvable when you simply recognize the limited premise at the heart of the perspective.

And when you do, you will find all of your answers there too.

Is this love?

Close your eyes and think of something you're currently worrying about.

When you worry about it, what story do you see in your mind? Close your eyes and let all of your worst fears unfold.

What if what you were worried about never happened? What do you see? Close your eyes and let that unfold.

Worrying creates events. You can see this first in your mind. When you're worrying, you are literally creating troubling outcomes, which you then experience over and over—as if they're actually happening—often causing yourself great suffering.

Worrying then goes on to create the experiences you're worried about, because while you're worrying, you are on high alert, looking for evidence, so you can either run away or fight. This is because your brain is designed to make connections that help you to survive by pointing out danger.

For example, if you repeatedly worry about getting sick from food poisoning, you probably did get sick that way once, and it was really miserable. You were traumatized. So your brain makes the connection between "sick" and "bad food," and now it focuses on that danger—instead of the tens of thousands of times you ate something and *didn't* get sick. Now you don't even *notice* those times, which far outweigh the sick times.

Because of "danger," your brain now focuses on potential bad food everywhere, and the more you see it, imagine it, and believe it, the more you worry about it. Every time your stomach is slightly upset, your brain links it to your sensitivity to bad food—whether you actually had any bad food or not. You begin to believe that you're really sensitive to food—that becomes your story—and pretty soon you're a basket case of worry and sensitivity. Worry creates the story you're worried about.

Sometimes the brain makes danger connections between events that are completely illogical. For example, if your paycheck fell out of your pocket on the first day you wore your new coat, your brain may connect those two unrelated events and create "anxiety" and "bad luck" whenever you wear that coat, as if it were the coat's fault you lost your check. Anything else "bad" that happens while you're wearing that coat just confirms what you knew all along—and pretty soon that coat ends up in the very back of your closet, never to see the light of day again.

But the stories you *don't* worry about usually don't happen. In fact, in your life there is an infinite number of stories that haven't and won't happen. But you don't notice this, because when things are going well, your brain goes off-line until there's "danger."

We hold on to worry as a protective measure—we tell ourselves that if we worry, we'll be more prepared for the bad thing when it happens. But worry creates stories that cause us tremendous suffering. In fact, most human suffering is caused not by actual events, but by the stories we create about ourselves.

Your life experiences are a direct reflection of what's happening in your mind. When you catch yourself worrying, try focusing your attention instead on all the times when you are just fine. Gradually, peace of mind can become your overwhelming condition.

Next time you find yourself worrying, consider this: Worrying is not the result of events. It is the cause. While you are worrying about the house burning down, you are actually visualizing the event and looking for signs of it everywhere.

And this reveals the deepest truth about worry—it isn't protection, it's *planning*. . . .

Meanwhile if the house is really burning down, there is nothing to worry about it—there's just something to *do*.

Do you remember a time that you branched out on your own, did something independently, disagreed with what everyone was saying, or spoke out? What happened?

How did it feel? Close your eyes and see where you go.

Is there something you could have known at the time that would have made it easier?

Go inside and see what comes up.

Is there something now?

What would make it easier?

Go in.

Nobody's watching.

This is a brain scan.

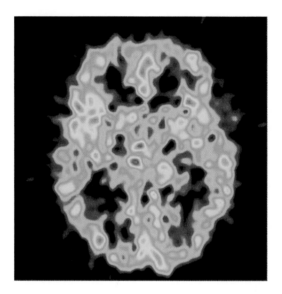

Close your eyes and see if you can feel any part of your body. When you do, let your attention rest there for a moment.

What happens when you do this? Do you feel any sensations? Do you see anything?

Close your eyes, do it again, and notice what happens.

Our brain is constantly scanning every cell of the body, and itself, in order to make the necessary microadjustments. This scanning mechanism is exponentially more powerful than any mechanical scanners in medicine, and most of our internal scans are accomplished by our brain completely without our conscious awareness. But it is possible to harness this power by simply putting your attention on any part of your body and feeling what is there.

Press your feet into the ground
and feel the bottom of your feet.

Feel your lungs breathing in and out.

Hold your hand in front of your mouth
and feel the breath on your skin.

Go inside and focus on those sensations,
and just notice where you go next.

We live in a Peekaboo universe.

The game of peekaboo is a real concept. You think you've fooled the baby into believing that you can't see him. But in fact, he's fooling you.

So far, the baby can only "see" and recognize the things he has been *taught* to identify. He has a long process ahead, of learning what to expect from things. In the meantime he is probably mostly aware of a kind of soup of information around him that pops in and out of existence, but has no real substance until he can "see" it by learning what things are and mean. The main thing he knows is that when he cries, a bottle magically appears. As far as he is concerned, he made that happen out of nothing—so he might feel pretty powerful. His world may feel like a loose and wavy place into which he can truly disappear and become part of the whole.

Perhaps babies "feel" a natural sense of what science has demonstrated: that everything in the universe is vibrating and spinning. Even the most solid cement sidewalks and rocky mountains and breakfast tables are made up of spiraling, vibrating particles. All of it creates a sound that we can't hear—but the universe is literally making music. It is possible that very young children are much more aware of that. They haven't learned to interpret all that spinning energy into things that they can recognize.

Not only that, but the atoms, which everything in the universe is made of, are mostly empty space. Our human body is an illusion, for like the cosmos, we, too, are mostly vast, empty space. If you could remove all the empty space from our bodies, everything that's left could fit into a small spoon.

In the game of peekaboo, when you hide your eyes or turn away from the baby, you tell yourself that of course he will still be there when you open your eyes. But that is an assumption based on the brain's tendency to fill in all the gaps with familiar memories and information—that things and people don't usually disappear quickly.

So, how do you really know *where* the baby went when you weren't looking?

We live in a sliver of awareness on the horizon of all thought.
Above us is all knowledge of everything.
Below us is fear and ignorance.
There is just as much thought below in the dark nether regions of
fear as there is above in the realm of light and knowledge.
We call this sliver of awareness of all thought "humanity."
Yet like the thoughts that you are aware of,
both realms of thought are always at work producing
what you experience.
What you're doing here with this book, and here on Earth, is
expanding your sliver of awareness
to encompass more of both the dark and the light—
the ignorance and the knowledge—
and thus becoming more aware of what thoughts you have,
and how they produce your existence.
As you bring the light of your awareness to the darkness,
it dissolves and becomes light.
This is why you can bring light to darkness, such as when the
darkness of a room dissipates with the flame of light from a candle,
but you can not bring darkness to light.
So as you become aware of all thought,
you become knowledge itself.

IMAGE APPENDIX

Page

vi. Michelanfelo's *David*, isolated. Copyright snem. Stockxpert.

xviii. *Raindrops Falling on Pond*. Close-up. Michael Banks. Digital Vision. Getty Images.

5. *Hand Holding Sun*. Dani Simmonds. Stockxchange. www.artfulscribe .org.

6. *Buddha with Flower*. Copyright Hanna Solin. www.HannaSolin.com.

7. *Twitch*. Copyright 2007, Hanna Solin. www.HannaSolin.com.

8. *Shine*. Brian Vezina. Workbook Stock. Jupiter Images. www.Jupiterimages .com. Also contact Brian@rhythmoflifephotography.com.

9. *Girl with Puppy*. Christopher Nutter.

10. *Sandbox Pyramid*. Christopher Nutter.

11. *Moon*. Copyright 2005, Miroslaw Okon. Contact: miroslawnyc@aol .com.

13. *Polar Bear*. Photo courtesy of the Commonwealth Club of California. The Commonwealth Club of California is the nation's oldest and largest public affairs forum, organizing more than 450 annual events on topics ranging across politics, culture, society, and the economy. A nonprofit, nonpartisan organization, the Commonwealth Club is based in San Francisco. Contact: www.commonwealthclub.org.

14. *Money Tree*. Copyright 2008, Arthur Solin.

17. *Masai Woman.* Copyright 2004, Robert S. Mauck. Contact: www .bobmauck.com.

18. *Aurora Borealis.* Phil Hart. www.philhart.com. Also, special thanks to Dark Sky Association: Dedicated to preserving the dark places in the world, so that we can continue to see the stars. Contact: www .DarkSky.org.

19. *Judging Fingers.* Copyright Hanna Solin and Mashid Mohadjerin.

20. *Flying Dice.* yblaz. Stockxpert.

22. *Wild Horse on the Beach.* Larissa Kisner. Donated by Corolla Wild Horse Fund, Inc., Karen McCalpin, Executive Director. Corolla Wild Horse Fund mission is to protect, preserve, and responsibly manage the herd of one hundred wild Colonial Spanish Mustangs roaming freely on the northernmost Currituck Outer Banks, and to promote the continued preservation of this land as a permanent sanctuary for horses defined as a cultural treasure by the state of North Carolina. For more information on how you can help, visit www.corollawildhorses.com.

23. *The Blue Marble.* NASA, public domain. http://visibleearth.nasa.gov.

24. *Maria con Hannibal.* Copyright Hanna Solin. www.HannaSolin.com.

25. *Poissons clown noirs.* Copyright 2008, Carine Vermenot.

26. 9/11 *Nebula.* NASA public domain. www.Hubblesite.org.

28. *Hands Drawing.* David Dykstra. www.DavidDykstra.com.

29. *Lightning.* Copyright 2007, Jason Lockwood. Jason.lockwood@talk21 .com. Special thanks to Cloud Appreciation Society: http://www .CloudAppreciationSociety.org.

32. *Sunrise Reflecting in Fog-Covered Lake.* Stockbyte. Photographer: Visions of America/Joe Sohm. PunchStockImages.

34. *Catherine Coats.* Christopher Nutter.

35. *Iraqi Girl with Leukemia,* Baghdad, Iraq. Copyright 2003, Alissa Everett. Alissa Everett Photography. www.AlissaEverett.com. Alissa Everett is founder and board member of Care Through Action (www .carethroughaction.org), a nonpartisan grassroots organization funding global change through local action, by raising awareness of and financial support for women and children suffering in some of the world's worst crises, beginning with Darfur.

36. *Children at Play,* Maldives, 2004. Copyright 2004, Alissa Everett. Alissa Everett Photography. www.AlissaEverett.com.

38. *Shattered Mirror.* Copyright 2008, Mashid Mohadjerin and Hanna Solin.

42. *Rigid. Life on Earth Does Not Require Compromise.* Copyright 2008, Linda Lauby. www.LindaLauby.com.

43. *Moo.* Christopher Nutter.

44. *Hands of God.* Copyright Joshua Black. iStockphoto.

46. *Leopard in Tree.* Copyright 2004, Robert Mauck. www.bobmauck.com.

48. *Her Director* (Series: Projections), 2000. Copyright 2000, Stephanie Annette Foxx. All rights reserved. www.stephaniefoxxstudio.com.

52. *Homeless Man.* Christopher Nutter.

54. *Rainbow.* Jacques Marie Francillon. Contact: jmfrancillon@orange.fr. Special thanks to Cloud Appreciation Society: www.CloudAppreciation Society.org.

55. *There Is.* Watercolor by Hanna Solin. www.HannaSolin.com.

57. *Mirror Me.* Copyright 2008, Bobbi Van. http://bobbivanstudio.com. Unfettered emotions, wild abandon . . . joy. My inner child rejoices. I have everything.

58. *Scenic Road Near Big Piney.* Copyright 2002, Conor Watkins. cwatkin@umr.edu.

59. *Infinity.* Copyright 2007, Sven Geier. This is a fractal. Visit his awesome Web site: www.SGeier.net.

61. *Ethiopian Mother with Son Dying of Malnutrition, Ethiopia.* Copyright 2005, Alissa Everett. Alissa Everett Photography. www.AlissaEverett.com. Also visit www.carethroughaction.org.

63. *Babies' Babies* (Series: Story of My Life), 2007. Copyright 2007, Stephanie Annette Foxx. All rights reserved. www.stephaniefoxxstudio.com.

68. *Waving.* Copyright 2008, Hanna Solin.

70. *Jail Hands.* Louates. Stockxchange.

71. *Belly Laugh.* Copyright 2007, Laurie York. Contact: www.LaurieYork Photography.com.

75. *Beach Scene.* Lori Coats.

79. *Ronin.* Christopher Nutter.

81. *Cancer Cell.* Copyright Sebastian Kaulitzki Eraxion. iStockphoto.

84. *Black Box.* Dean Franklin.

86. *Cat's Eye.* NASA, public domain. www.HubbleSite.org.

88. *Sophie and Denda.* Jim Schulz, photographer. (Special thanks to Jim Schulz and Carol Sodaro at Brookfield Zoo for this magnificent photograph.) Copyright Chicago Zoological Society/Brookfield Zoo, Chicago, IL. Special thanks to Christine Mallar at the Orangutan Conservancy: www.orangutan.net. Orangutan Foundation: www.orangutan.org.

89. *A Field of Sunflowers Facing the sun.* Soupstock. Stockxpert.

92. *Palestinian Boy with Rifle, Gaza Strip, 2002.* Copyright Alissa Everett. Alissa Everett Photography. www.AlissaEverett.com.

94. *Smiling Bottlenose Dolphin.* Copyright 2008, Eric Cheng. http://echeng.com.

95. *Paul Inspired.* Copyright 2005, Luc Edouard Georges. www.LucGeorges.com.

96. *Pink Elephant05.* Copyright Frederick Matzen, Dreamstime.com.

98. *Rhett.* Jason Nutter.

99. *Spaghetti.* Copyright 2008, Atila Marquez. www.atilamarquez.com.

101. *Spiral Arms.* NASA, public domain. HubbleSite.org.

102. *Elephants3.* Susanna Altarriba. Stockxpert. Mail to: Casacentelles.telefonica.net Also, special thanks to Sheldrick Wildlife Trust (www.Sheldrickwildlifetrust.org), committed to the rescue, care, and rehabilitation of orphaned baby elephants and rhinos in West Africa.

103. *Your Story Chalkboard.* Copyright 2008, Mashid Mohadjerin and Hanna Solin.

104. *Baby Partridge.* Copyright Eric Brust. Stockxpert.

106. *Open 24 Hours.* Copyright 2008, Hanna Solin.

109. *Upload Button.* Copyright 2008, Kristin Smith.

110. *The Milky Way over the Dark Skies of the New Mexico Desert.* Chris Cook. Photo Researchers, Inc. Special thanks to Dark Sky Association, dedicated to preserving the dark places in the world, so that we can continue to see the stars. www.DarkSky.org.

112. *Tally Marks on Wall.* Copyright 2008, Mashid Mohadjerin.

114. *Catherine Coats in Mirror.* Copyright 2008, Atila Marquez. http://atilamarquez.com. (Adapted from *The Grand System* exercise developed by David Grand, Ph.D.)

116. *A Surfer Hits the Top of a Wave and Appears to Fly.* PixelChik. Stockxpert. Also, special thanks to Corolla Surf Shop: www.CorollaSurfShop.com.

119. *Shiite Men Praying for Ashoura, Beirut, Lebanon, 2004.* Copyright 2004, Alissa Everett. Alissa Everett Photography. www.AlissaEverett.com. Also visit www.carethroughaction.org.

120. *Old Woman/Young Woman.* Public domain. Originally a German postcard, circa 1880, of anonymous origin.

121. *Money Out of Pocket.* Paulgeor. Stockxpert.

122. *Deep Dive.* Copyright 2007, Sven Geier. This image is a fractal. Visit his beautiful fractal Web site. www.SGeier.net.

126. *NYC Radical Fairy.* Luc Georges. www.lucgeorges.com.

129. *Abandoned Wheelchair.* Copyright 2008, Paul Gallo. ww.no3rdw.com.

130. *Native American Headdress.* Copyright 2008, Carine Vermenot.

133. *Antarctic Ice Caves.* Copyright 2007, Staphy. Stockxpert.

135. *People Walking Through Maze of Paper, Man Flying Above Them.* Stockbyte. Getty Images.

136. *Evil Face.* Copyright Ivan Pernjakovic/Dreamstime.com. www .Dreamstime.com.

137. *Reverse Stop.* Copyright 2008, Hanna Solin.

138. *Dance Brazil.* Copyright Nan Melville. www.nanmelville.com. Also, special thanks to Mestre Jelon Vieira. www.dancebrazil.org.

140. *Remote Control.* Copyright ishook. Stockxpert.

141. *Frenzy/The Contortionist.* Copyright 2008, Bruce Waldman. www .BruceWaldman.com.

142. *Liza Booth.* Christopher Nutter.

144. *Casket Side View on Black.* the cartinko. iStockphoto.

145. *Cubicle.* Copyright 2008, Kristin Smith. Smith and Westbrook.

146. *Nuclear Bomb Test*, Nevada, June 18, 1957. Digital Vision. Getty Images.

148. *Orange.* Dean Franklin.

149. *Sad Dog in Cage.* Kim Ruane, photographer. Pictured is Skippy, adopted from the Monmouth County SPCA in April 2006. Monmouth County SPCA, Eatontown, NJ, 732-542-0040. www.monmouthcountyspca.org. The Monmouth County Society for Prevention of Cruelty to Animals is a nonprofit organization that was founded in 1945. Each year, the organization cares for nearly four thousand companion animals who need a safe haven while they await their "forever" homes. At the

Monmouth County SPCA, each adoptable animal, like Skippy, is given all the time he or she needs to find the right home.

150. *Ménage à Trois.* Copyright 2008, Carine Vermenot.

151. *Tahitian Paradise.* Copyright 2008, Carine Vermenot.

152. *Darfur Refugees Waiting for Registration*, Eastern Chad, 2006. Copyright 2006 Alissa Everett. Alissa Everett Photography. www.AlissaEverett .com. Also visit www.carethroughaction.org.

153. *Echo Lake.* Copyright 2008, Carine Vermenot.

155. *Mirror Oval.* Stockbyte. Getty Images.

156. *Star Cluster.* NASA, public domain. www.Hubblesite.org.

158. *Floating Island.* Copyright Roben Ponce. To see more work, go to www .photoshoptalent.com/profile/Island_Boy/&view.

160. *Relax.* Copyright 2008, Christopher Nutter.

161. *Iridescent Gelatin Capsules on Bright Blue Background.* Chris Knapton. Photdisk. Getty Images.

166. *Rattlesnake.* Copyright 2008, Carine Vermenot.

170. *Bee Swarm.* Henry Firus. Flagstaffotos. www.flagstaffotos.com.au.

171. *Horus 11.* Copyright 2008, Carine Vermenot. This unretouched photograph is of a wild hawk (named Horus) who landed on the photographer's fire escape and stayed for eight hours, while allowing her to photograph him from only two feet away with her window wide open. (Hawk symbolism: The hawk is called messenger, protector, and visionary. Keen vision is one of its greatest gifts. Hawks see things others miss. They can teach you how to fly high while keeping yourself connected to the ground. If a hawk has soared into your life, you require a higher perspective.)

173. *Crop Circle, Triple Julia Set. Windmill Hill, 1996.* Copyright 1996, Freddy Silva. Best-selling author of *Secrets in the Fields: The Science and Mysticism of Crop Circles.* Visit: www.invisibletemple.com.

174. *Insurance Won't Cover This* (Series: Open Hearts), 2004. Copyright 2004, Stephanie Annette Foxx. All rights reserved. www.stephaniefoxx studio.com.

176. *Merging Galaxies.* NASA, public domain. www.HubbleSite.org.

178. *Silhouette of Depression.* Copyright 2006, Robbie L. Rodrigues.

181. *Sheep Eating Grass.* Henry Firus. Flagstaffotos. www.flagstaffotos.com.au.

184. *Brain Scan.* Copyright 2008, P. Reigh LeBlanc.

185. *Butterfly 1.* Copyright 2008, Carine Vermenot.

186. *Peekaboo Mother and Baby.* Copyright 2008, Charlie Sedanayasa. sedanayasa@hotmail.com. http://flickr.com/photos/sedanayasa.

189. *Whale Breaching.* Copyright 2008, Carine Vermenot.

190. *Child in the Sea.* Image Source. Punchstock Images.

ACKNOWLEDGMENTS, CHRISTINE RANCK

I would like to gratefully acknowledge the following people, whose love, patience, guidance, and support have carried me through these past few years. This book would have never come into being without you.

Christopher Nutter, my writing partner and friend, whose creative genius forever inspires me, and without whom this book would never have gotten out of my mind and onto paper. With our third eye, together we've lovingly made a whole that is much greater than the sum of its parts. And to Sagi Haviv, artist, genius, and dear friend, who synchronistically brought us together, and then produced the masterpiece that was our book proposal.

To David Grand, soundtrack creator, my teacher, mentor, creative inspiration, and dear friend. You have positively changed and influenced the course of my life in every way it is possible to influence another person. I will never be able to adequately thank you for your love, generosity, and support.

To my wonderful family: my husband, Rich, whose steadiness, integrity, love, and commitment have been a beacon of strength for me for half of my life. I know how lucky I am. To my parents, Robert and Sue, you have given me the strength, stability, and courage to believe in myself enough to do this. To my brother Stephen and his children, my nephews Paul, Chris, and Andy; to Jane, to my sister Susan, brother-in-law Scott, and my nieces Hannah and Sophia; to my brother Gregg and my nephews Justin and Evan; to my brother Richard, sister-in-law Rachel, and their children Emily, Ian, Evie, Eli, and Elly. To my beloved aunts, Barbara and Dorothy, and all my cousins.

To my stepchildren, Richie, Kenny, Jean, and Diana, whom I love dearly. Thank you for so generously welcoming me into your lives. To their spouses Michele, Keith, and Jimmy, and to my grandchildren, Ryan, Lauren, Angelina, Kenny, Tyler, Max, Katie, Gavin, and Jamie, all of whom I adore. You are all part of the most wonderful and supportive family a person could ever hope to have and I love you all more than you will ever know.

To Brenda Tepper, my mother away from home, whose steady love and integrity inspired my growth over the many years that I have counted on you; to Natalie Rogers, my other mother away from home, who introduced me to EMDR and who, with her love and colossal strength, encouraged my creativity.

To the Interlochen Music Camp in Traverse City, Michigan, where I learned I could sing and my life was never the same again. To Miss Stimpfle, speech teacher in 1967 at Worthington High School, who taught me how to be a public speaker and actress. To the Baldwin School where I grew up and learned how to write. To the Institute for Contemporary Psychotherapy, for giving me an incredible education that prepared me for the privilege of becoming a psychotherapist.

To my beloved singing girlfriends Sula Haska (you are my oak tree) and Patti Wyss, who have shared so many years of making beautiful music together as *Jukebox Jane*, thank you for your love and support. To my also beloved girlfriends Martha Schut, Therese Collins, Kim Ruane, Leigh Stewart, Serena Silva, Rosanna Chavez, Patty Ewald, Nancy D'Aurizio, Donna Consolini, Helen Adrienne, Mary Ellen Tormey, Martha Jacobi, Gwen Hawkes Jackson, Ronni Kuchar, Toy Dupres, Jeannette Gardner, and Lisa Schwarz, without whom my life would be very empty. I don't know how to thank you and I love you dearly. To my friend Barbara Barr McDaniel, whom I've loved since boarding school, who single-handedly introduced me to show business and the possibility of living a creative life: You have influenced me more than you could ever know. To my beloved friends Jeff Ambers, Peter Poliakine, Mauricio Bustamante, Jamie Rocco, Albert Evans, Dennis Deal, Donn Ruddy, Arnold Barcena, Doug Peters, Lee Ielpi, Ed Cionek, Bruce Waldman, Randy Hugill, Richard Joelson, Rob Kuchar, and Rob Polishook, artists and humans of unbelievable talent, and steadfast friends through all the many years. To Mike Lobel, friend, artist, and recording genius. To Mark Planner, my incredible voice teacher and friend. To Elyce Kirsch for sharing laughs and love at endless conferences. To Laurie Delaney, whose friendship, support, and generosity have been a beacon for me in too many situations to even count.

To my Supervision Group, extraordinary therapists and human beings all: Kathleen Brown-McNally, Cynthia Schwartz-berg, Sue Pinco, Deborah Antinori, Barbara Hennessey, Dan Gates, David Sherwood, Beppe Manca (and Liliana), Goldie Meyer, Kathryn Gallagher, and Ira Dressner. Thank you for listening to my ideas and encouraging me to keep going. Your support has been invaluable.

To Abigail Brenner, whose support and friendship have been irreplaceable. Thank you for including me in your beautiful book, *Women's Rites of Passage.* To Judith Adler, creative powerhouse. To Kathy Chetkovich, writer, artist, and editor, who helped me to clarify my thoughts and express myself in the early days of this book.

To Carol Pavitt, friend, painter, and artist, who synchronistically led me to my first quantum physics book and encouraged me to write my dissertation.

To my Creativity Support Group: Dominique Plaisant, Kristin Smith, Campbell Hatcher, and Eric DySart, all creative geniuses and gifted artists who helped me to formulate my ideas.

To the International Women's Writing Guild, where I honed my writing skills, and joined a spectacular community of women writers.

To Hanna Solin, Creative Being, for her magnificent creative gifts, and whose skills and artistry saved me and this book more than once.

To David Toney, actor colossus and dear friend, who introduced me to my first holographic experience when he stepped into the role of Othello before my very eyes. Your talent and loving spirit have inspired me.

To Joe and the team at Giacomo's on 72nd and West End for feeding me practically every meal I ate during this whole process.

To Melissa Miller, capable, kind, sweet, intelligent, irreplaceable support in the creation of this book.

To Amy Hertz, our awesome editor, for choosing our book

against all the odds, for having the clarity and wisdom to see its potential, and for supporting us in the challenging and thrilling process of making a book.

To Art Kara, who created our beautiful, classy, and perfect cover design.

To all of the staff at Penguin Group and others who worked hard to make this book a success.

To Amy Hughes, our agent, and a prodigious writing talent herself, for inestimable support, talent, and capabilities, whose strength and giftedness got us where we needed to get.

To all the artists and photographers and wonderful organizations who donated their art to this project, and whose generosity will always be appreciated.

To the rest of my family and friends, I feel blessed to have the abundance of your love and support.

And finally, thank you to my clients; you have been a major source of inspiration to me. I am so grateful for your confidence in me, and for the unparalleled privilege of knowing your stories and witnessing your courage. Your openness and commitment to personal renewal forever remind me of why I chose to work in this field.

ACKNOWLEDGMENTS, CHRIS NUTTER

I would like to thank Christine Ranck who, from the first moment I sat down on her couch as her client, and then as her coauthor, has expanded my consciousness and my art to levels I had never thought to imagine; David Grand for producing the audio soundtrack that accompanies this book, which not only made the method Christine and I developed together possible but which has literally changed the way I think; my agent Amy Hughes at McCormick & Williams, who, in procuring and editing my first book, *The Way Out: The Gay Man's Guide to Freedom,* and in so brilliantly and deftly placing this one, has at this point in my life done as much to advance my career and ensure that my vision makes it to the public as anyone; Sagi Haviv at Chermayeff & Geismar, who designed the proposal (and the Web site) for this book with the hand of a true artistic genius, creating the template for it and thus the template for the very method; Amy Hertz at Penguin for showing such bold editorial farsightedness in bringing it under her wing and great reverence for the words and ideas of her writers; Melissa Miller at Penguin for working so selflessly and brilliantly to coordinate the enormous number of details involved with this getting this book to press and on the shelves; my incredible team of nonphysical entities who channeled profound wisdom through me into this book and into my life, and finally my mother, Betty, who created a library out of our house and nurtured me with books, demonstrating to me firsthand what it is to show love with words.